"Resources made by and for people of color who are looking to grow in contemplative Christian practices are few and far between, but Made for Pax is an oasis in a spiritual desert. Their commitment to empowering and raising up voices as part of the global majority is a testament to their shalom-filled activism. The Made for Pax Bible Studies are thoughtful resources for folks who are passionate about fostering the flourishing of all."
Jenai Auman, writer and author of *Othered*

"We long for integrity—in ourselves, in society, in the church. I love how the Made for Pax Bible Studies embody integrity in both what they present and how they present it. Addressing important topics often neglected by the church, these books call us to live out a holistic faith—and do so by engaging us holistically as readers. Here are pages filled with poems, prayers, visual art, embodied practices, and more, inviting us to join Jesus step by step, breath by breath, in the work of cultivating integrity and shalom in ourselves and in the world."
Michael Stalcup, poet

"The Made for Pax Bible Study Series is a gift for anyone seeking contemplative scriptural learning. These well-structured studies offer engaging writing and thoughtfully chosen topics. The units on mental health and migration are particularly timely and important, addressing crucial contemporary issues. This is a valuable resource for those seeking deeper understanding, centering often decentered voices."
Guesnerth Josué Perea, director of Black Lives and Contemplation for the Community of the Incarnation

"The Made for Pax Bible Study *Mental Health* is an incredibly rich, layered, and compassionate mental health offering. Each week lovingly weaves insights from science, Scripture, art, contemplation, justice, and more to help create a tapestry of hope for the reader that is ultimately rooted in the kindness and nearness of God. I'm so grateful this resource exists."
Aundi Kolber, licensed professional counselor and author of *Try Softer* and *Strong like Water*

MENTAL HEALTH

Experiencing God's Care for Our Mind, Body, and Spirit

A 6-WEEK INTERACTIVE BIBLE STUDY

DORCAS CHENG-TOZUN

InterVarsity Press
P.O. Box 1400 | Downers Grove, IL 60515-1426
ivpress.com | email@ivpress.com

Written by Dorcas Cheng-Tozun

InterVarsity Press® is the publishing division of InterVarsity Christian Fellowship/USA®. For more information, visit intervarsity.org.

Published in association with Joy Eggerichs Reed of Punchline Agency.

Cover design: Faceout Studio, Tim Green
Interior design: Nat Maxey
Cover images: © CSA-Printstock / DigitalVision Vectors via Getty Images and © CSA Images via Getty Images
Interior images: Made for Pax

ISBN 978-1-5140-1290-1 (print) | ISBN 978-1-5140-1291-8 (digital)

Printed in the United States of America ♾

Library of Congress Cataloging-in-Publication Data
A catalog record for this book is available from the Library of Congress.

30 29 28 27 26 25 | 8 7 6 5 4 3 2 1

CONTENTS

If you or someone you know is in a life-threatening situation, please make use of the resources below, which are available 24/7:

National Suicide Prevention Lifeline
1-800-273-8255 | https://suicidepreventionlifeline.org/chat/ (online chat)

Substance Abuse and Mental Health Services Administration
1-800-662-4357 (treatment referral and information)

National Youth Crisis Hotline
1-800-448-4663 (interventions for sexual abuse, child abuse, depression, and suicidal thoughts)

Welcome

Welcome to this six-week study on mental health!

This course takes you on a deep exploration of how we can experience God's love and presence in our mental health journeys. By the time you complete all six sessions of this study, you will: (1) understand how God sees our mental health, and how that differs from what we often hear in the church, (2) learn how Jesus suffers alongside us and seeks to redeem our mental health struggles, and (3) gain practical, God-honoring tools and approaches to help care for our own mental health and that of others.

Mental health is a key topic that young Christians want to know about yet are challenged to find relevant, thoughtful, biblically based resources that answer their questions. This study includes a diverse collection of Jesus-centered art, scholarship, and storytelling, primarily created by people of color, that provides teaching, guidance, and opportunities for reflection. In addition to studying Scripture, you will also read essays and personal testimonies, experience spoken word and poetry, meditate on visual art, and listen to or watch in-depth interviews and panels. We hope you will experience a spiritual feast for your senses and your soul, inspiring you in your journey to learn more about the character of God and the discipleship he calls each of us to.

Psalm 121
BY MONDO SCOTT
PSALM
121:1,2
I LIFT MY EYES UP, TO THE MOUNTAINS - WHERE DOES MY HELP COME FROM?
MY HELP COMES FROM YOU, MAKER OF HEAVEN, CREATOR OF THE EARTH

HOW TO USE THIS STUDY

Below is a breakdown of the study structure and approach. The opening and closing sessions are distinct from the middle four sessions and have less content to allow for more discussion and reflection. In each session, you will also engage with unique audio and video content. Scan the accompanying QR code on each page to access the digital material.

Session 1	**Opening**	Introduces the topic of mental health and creates space to reflect on initial ideas, teachings, questions, and doubts that may surface.
Session 2	**Manifesto**	Overviews approaches to mental health and explores the foundational spiritual truth that guides the rest of the sessions.
Session 3	**Myth**	Names and deconstructs common false beliefs and teachings about mental health within church and society.
Session 4	**Material**	Delves into Jesus-centered, biblically based teachings on mental health and its implications for how we live.
Session 5	**Motion**	Explores meaningful ways to embrace healthy, relevant embodied practices in our everyday lives.
Session 6	**Closing**	Reviews the main themes from the study and facilitates next steps to apply learnings in practical and meaningful ways.

Opening Session

The Opening session begins with (1) a pulse check to gauge where participants are coming from at the start of the study, followed by (2) an introduction to the overall study. Then you will engage (3) an excerpt of a conversation about mental health and (4) the four path point statements, or the overarching themes of the study, along with a holy imagination exercise, before closing with (5) a benediction and (6) an application activity.

Sessions 2–5

You will (1) preview the focus for the week and (2) read the path point statement and a brief reflection that frames the content of the session. Then you will study (3) a passage of Scripture and (4) additional content from a relevant expert. Each session concludes with (5) a communal benediction and (6) an application activity for the week to encourage further learning and embodied action.

Closing Session

The Closing session provides (1) a review of the content in the entire study and gives space to (2) revisit and reflect upon the path point statements previously studied. Then, you will (3) consider ways to build faith communities that embrace those who struggle with mental health, and (4) identify practical ways to extend love and care to those who are hurting. You will end your time together with (5) a prayer and benediction.

OUR DISCIPLESHIP PATHWAY

The four path points of the discipleship pathway—Manifesto, Myth, Material, and Motion—help us unpack one big idea from concept to call to action. These path points are the stepping stones that guide our journey with Jesus, God's Spirit, and each other as we consider how peacemaking impacts our approach to mental health.

MANIFESTO—Declaration of Peace

Proclaim the good news of peace in the world.

MYTH—Distortion of Peace

Discern the lies and false narratives that surround us.

MATERIAL—Expressions of Peace

Reveal the scriptural witness of peace in the world.

MOTION—Embodiment of Peace

Participate in the active work of peace in the world.

SESSION 1 Opening

We're so glad you have chosen to participate in this six-week study on how God is with us in our mental health journeys!

In this first session, we will learn about mental health, including the mental health challenges that many face and how they fit within our spiritual lives. We'll spend time reflecting on what we've been taught about mental health and how that has influenced our own perspectives. We'll also introduce the path point statements (which are like thesis statements) that we will focus on throughout the study. This session sets up the framework through which we will view the topic of mental health.

As defined by the US Department of Health and Human Services, *"Mental health includes our emotional, psychological, and social well-being. It affects how we think, feel, and act. It also helps determine how we handle stress, relate to others, and make choices. Mental health is important at every stage of life, from childhood and adolescence through adulthood."*

REFLECTION

As we begin to consider the notion of mental health, take about fifteen minutes to consider the following reflection questions.

1. When you think of mental health, what are the first associations that come to mind?

2. Have you ever heard mental health discussed in Christian churches, organizations, or social circles? If yes, what opinions, ideas, and teachings did you hear? If not, why do you think mental health hasn't been addressed?

3. How do you think our mental health intersects with our spirituality and our relationship with God? What questions do you have about this?

INTRODUCTION

In the United States, at least one in five adults struggles with mental health; as many as one-third of individuals will have an anxiety disorder at some point in their lives. Recent studies suggest these numbers may be rising. Perhaps you or someone you know has experienced this form of suffering.

Mental health and religion have a long history of being intertwined together. Ancient peoples believed that mental health disorders were caused by demon possession or divine punishment. The perspective began to change around 400 BC, when Greek physician Hippocrates treated mental health issues as physiological illnesses. But, many centuries and scientific discoveries later, those ancient religious beliefs continue to persist, affecting how we perceive mental health and perceive those who face emotional hardships today.

For the most part, the modern church has a terrible track record of judging and marginalizing those who struggle with mental health. But this treatment has never reflected God's heart—in ancient times or today. A close examination of Scripture shows us narrative after narrative of psychologically vulnerable individuals. We see depression in Elijah, Naomi, Jeremiah, and Jonah; we see anxiety in Moses, David, Jesus, and the disciples. And these same individuals are seen, loved, embraced, and called by God. Their vulnerabilities did not bar them from the presence, will, or plan of God. Instead, we see God responding to their struggles with tenderness and compassion, and filling their lives with purpose.

God wants to bring beauty, hope, and purpose to each of us. God wants to give us his very presence in every facet of our mental health journeys.

PERSONAL STORY

Open, honest conversations about mental health don't tend to happen as often as they should. As a result, we can internalize ideas that cause us to neglect, dismiss, or harm our own mental health. These misguided ideas can come from our families, communities, churches, and media.

Watch a brief excerpt of a conversation between PAX staff members Dorcas Cheng-Tozun and Osheta Moore, who have both lived with anxiety and depression. Start at 7:50 and end at 10:11. Then respond to the reflection questions below.

"How Mental Health Struggles Changed Me"

WITH DORCAS CHENG-TOZUN AND OSHETA MOORE

REFLECTION

1. What messages have you heard in your families or churches that negatively impacted your mental health?

2. If we are to be compassionate and caring toward those with mental health challenges, what common theologies or beliefs within Christian circles do we need to challenge? What is a more loving and biblical approach to mental health?

PATH POINT STATEMENTS

Each step in our discipleship pathway has a statement that captures the main idea of that path point. We begin with an audacious truth (Manifesto) that will frame our entire study on mental health; then we move to address a common false belief (Myth) that impedes us from believing God's truth. We then focus on the word of God and person of Jesus to strengthen our theological understanding of mental health (Material), and conclude with practical ways in which God calls us to embody these truths in our everyday lives (Motion).

Read the four statements and answer the reflection question. Then pause and fill out the "what if" questions in the holy imagination exercise. You'll have the opportunity to share your responses.

MANIFESTO STATEMENT	Beauty and brokenness coexist in our stories.
MYTH STATEMENT	"Faith is all I need."
MATERIAL STATEMENT	Jesus experiences our mental health journey with us.
MOTION STATEMENT	Caring for our mental health is a sacred practice.

REFLECTION

Which of these statements sticks out most to you? Why? What is your initial response to it?

Holy Imagination Exercise

Christians throughout the ages have engaged their holy imagination, also called *faithful imagination*, to expand their capacity for understanding God and his kingdom. Because these Manifesto, Material, and Motion statements are true (and the Myth statement is categorically false), we can be empowered to imagine how our world might be different.

Take a few minutes to write out at least three "what if" statements that could be true if we recognized that God values our mental health, desires us to make use of the mental health resources available to us, and experiences our mental health journeys with us. (Examples: What if churches were uniquely safe and supportive environments for those who struggled with mental health challenges? What if we truly believed that Jesus understood and empathized with our mental health journeys?)

What if ?

What if ?

What if ?

What if ?

Share your statements with the group, as well as any thoughts or reflections this exercise prompted.

BENEDICTION

Mental health can feel like a deeply personal topic shrouded in shame and complexity. Yet God invites us to come to him with our greatest vulnerabilities, believing in God's gentle care and unconditional love. We don't know if our mental health journeys will involve full healing, partial healing, or no healing. But can we still believe that God is good and is doing good work in us?

Read this prayer from Jesuit priest Pierre Teilhard de Chardin, called "The Slow Work of God," to close your time this week.

Above all, trust in the slow work of God.
We are, quite naturally, impatient in everything to reach the end
Without delay.
We should like to skip
The intermediate stages.
We are impatient of being on
The way to something unknown,
Something new,
And yet it is the law of all progress
That it is made by passing through
Some stages of instability—
And that it may take a very long time.
And so I think it is with you.
Your ideas mature gradually—
Let them grow,
Let them shape themselves,
Without undue haste.
Don't try to force them on,
As though you could be today
What time will make you tomorrow.
Only God could say what this new spirit
Gradually forming within you will be.
Give Our Lord the benefit of believing
That his hand is leading you,
And accept the anxiety of
Feeling yourself in suspense and incomplete.

APPLICATION ACTIVITY

Scripture Reading and Reflection

Set aside fifteen minutes to read and reflect on 1 Kings 19:1-17. Below, trace the emotional journey of Elijah over these series of events, and consider how God responded. We will spend more time with this passage in the next session.

SESSION 2

Manifesto

DECLARATION OF PEACE

Last week, we began to examine how God is with us in the ups and downs of our mental health, and how the church has typically responded to mental health challenges. This session is all about the Manifesto path point, or the big idea we want to focus on. We will spend time with Scripture and an essay, both of which explore how God encourages us, made in God's image, to view mental health.

INTRODUCTION

Despite Jesus' clear teachings to the contrary (Matthew 5:10-11; John 15:19; 16:33), many followers of Jesus often expect that life will go smoothly for them. We may assume that we'll always have what we need, or that we'll always experience the deep peace of God.

And yet even the most faithful Christians are not exempt from human suffering—and that includes mental health challenges. Living with anxiety or depression or bipolar disorder is not, as some might assume, an indictment of our character or behavior. Jesus himself challenged these assumptions (John 9:3), and decades of scientific research show us that most mental health struggles are related to genetics, trauma, or our environment.

When we experience chemical imbalances or dysregulated neurological connections, we are not any less beloved or less representative of the image of God. Such suffering and heartache do not diminish the hope and beauty of our humanity or the presence of our sovereign God.

MANIFESTO STATEMENT

In the last session, we introduced the Manifesto statement, which provides the framework for today's Bible passage and essay. The Manifesto statement is a foundational truth that connects the dots between God, us, and mental health.

Read this statement and then pray a brief prayer to open your heart to what the Holy Spirit may want to teach you today.

Beauty and brokenness coexist in our stories.

SCRIPTURE READING

1 Kings 19:1-13, 15-16

Elijah was a prophet of God during a tumultuous time in Israel's history. King Ahab and Queen Jezebel had led the people far from God, worshiping false gods like Baal and Asherah, and massacring Yahweh's faithful prophets and ministers. Just prior to this passage, Elijah challenges Ahab and his false prophets to a public confrontation between their respective gods at Mount Carmel. The God of Israel shows up as all-consuming fire from heaven, and Elijah kills the prophets of Baal and Asherah in judgment. It is an unquestionable victory for Elijah—but his fortunes quickly change.

Read the passage below and then consider the reflection questions.

Ahab told Jezebel all that Elijah had done and how he had killed all the prophets with the sword. Then Jezebel sent a messenger to Elijah, saying, "So may the gods do to me and more also, if I do not make your life like the life of one of them by this time tomorrow." Then he was afraid; he got up and fled for his life and came to Beer-sheba, which belongs to Judah; he left his servant there.

But he himself went a day's journey into the wilderness and came and sat down under a solitary broom tree. He asked that he might die, "It is enough; now, O LORD, take away my life, for I am no better than my ancestors." Then he lay down under the broom tree and fell asleep. Suddenly an angel touched him and said to him, "Get up and eat." He looked, and there at his head was a cake baked on hot stones and a jar of water. He ate and drank and lay down again.

The angel of the LORD came a second time, touched him, and said, "Get up and eat, or the journey will be too much for you." He got up and ate and drank; then he went in the strength of that food forty days and forty nights to Horeb the mount of God. At that place he came to a cave and spent the night there.

Then the word of the LORD came to him, saying, "What are you doing here, Elijah?" He answered, "I have been very zealous for the LORD, the God of hosts, for the Israelites have forsaken your covenant, thrown down your altars, and killed your prophets with the sword. I alone am left, and they are seeking my life, to take it away."

He said, "Go out and stand on the mountain before the LORD, for the LORD is about to pass by." Now there was a great wind, so strong that it was splitting mountains and breaking rocks in pieces before the LORD, but the LORD was not in the wind, and after the wind an earthquake, but the LORD *was not in the earthquake, and after the earthquake a fire, but the* LORD *was not in the fire, and after the fire a sound of sheer silence. When Elijah heard it, he wrapped his face in his mantle and went out and stood at the entrance of the cave. . . .*

Then the LORD *said to him, "Go, return on your way to the wilderness of Damascus; when you arrive, you shall anoint Hazael as king over Aram. Also you shall anoint Jehu son of Nimshi as king over Israel, and you shall anoint Elisha son of Shaphat of Abel-meholah as prophet in your place."*

REFLECTION

1. How did Elijah move from faith and confidence on Mount Carmel to despair and a desire for death in the wilderness in such a short amount of time?

2. What are the various ways that God responds to Elijah? What does this demonstrate about the character of God?

ESSAY EXCERPT

Beauty and brokenness are intrinsic to the human experience, and as we saw with Elijah, God's people are not exempt. Yet God meets us in our struggles. In the essay below, theologian and mental health advocate Paul Lu explains that because God cares for our mental health, Christian communities should be safe, welcoming, and loving spaces for those facing mental health challenges.

Take a few minutes to read this essay excerpt. Then we'll discuss the reflection questions that follow.

"A Sound Theology of Mental Health"

BY PAUL LU

Some time ago, the mother of a child with a mental health disorder shared with me the frustrations she had experienced at her church. When she asked church leaders for support, they denied that her child had a mental disorder. And if anything was wrong, they said, the mother and child were to blame.

This is quite a common story at churches. The body of Christ, in general, is poorly equipped to respond to the mental health needs of their communities. And many families have been deeply hurt as a result. Churches and faith communities should be places of healing and hope, where those who struggle with mental health are welcomed with compassion, respect, and honor. But we can only do that when we develop a robust, God-centered perspective on mental health.

Today, mental disorders affect one in five adults, according to the National Alliance on Mental Illness. About 5 percent of adults, or one in twenty, experience serious mental illness.[1] In the United States alone, 40 million adults suffer from some form of anxiety; among those, nearly half have been diagnosed with a depressive disorder.[2] Mental health conditions are more prevalent among women compared to men, and 17 percent of youth aged six to seventeen have a mental health disorder. Fourteen percent of Asians, 17 percent of Blacks, 18 percent of Latino individuals, 32 percent of multiracial adults, and 44 percent of LGBTQ individuals experience mental disorders.[3] Mental health challenges impact those who are suffering, but also their family members and friends.

Contrary to the common teaching that "good" Christians should not struggle with "bad" mental health, followers of Jesus experience mental health challenges as much as the general population. We even see this in Scripture. For instance, Job says, "I am not at ease, nor am I quiet; I have no rest; but trouble comes" (Job 3:26). David, who wrote some of the most wrenching laments in the Bible, at one point cries out to God, "Come quickly, Lord, and answer me, for my depression deepens" (Psalm 143:6 NLT). And the prophet Elijah, as he runs for his life from Queen Jezebel, laments, "It is enough; now, O Lord, take away my life, for I am no better than my ancestors" (1 Kings 19:4).

In more recent times, mental health issues have continued to affect prominent leaders of the church. For instance, Martin Luther suffered from depression during his time as a monk.[4] Nineteenth-century theologian Charles Spurgeon also suffered from depression, which he said he would not wish on anyone.[5] Christian apologist J.P. Moreland tells of his battle with debilitating anxiety, including panic attacks, in his book *Finding Quiet: My Story of Overcoming Anxiety and the Practices that Brought Peace.*

PAUSE & REFLECT

Who are the other people in the Bible or church history who seem to have struggled with their mental or emotional heath?

Given how common mental health issues are among people, including Christians, we may wonder why a loving God would allow such suffering. The prophet Jeremiah expresses this sense of confusion and rejection: "But why, why this chronic pain, this ever worsening wound and no healing in sight? You're nothing, GOD, but a mirage, a lovely oasis in the distance—and then nothing!" (Jeremiah 15:18 MSG).

Amidst the pain and suffering, God does understand. Toward the end of the book of Jonah, the prophet declares, "And now, O LORD, please take my life from me, for it is better for me to die than to live." God does not condemn Jonah or become angry with him. Instead, the Lord engages Jonah, gently asking, "Is it right for you to be angry?" (Jonah 4:3-4). God could have given up on Jonah. But he is patient. He understands Jonah's frustration and doubts.

In the Gospel of John, Jesus encounters a man blind from birth. His disciples ask, "Rabbi, who sinned, this man or his parents, that he was born blind?" Jesus answers, "Neither this man nor his parents sinned; he was born blind so that God's works might be revealed in him" (John 9:1-3).

Jesus affirms that our illnesses and limitations are not a punishment for our sins or that of our parents. Having emotional disorders or other mental health challenges is not anyone's fault. Instead, it is so that we may be witnesses for God's goodness. The Lord's unconditional love and wise purposes are not diminished for those with mental health challenges. ***Instead of looking to blame, judge, or shame those who are struggling, we should look for the image of God, and evidence of his work, in that individual.***

This is not a promise that God will heal our mental health struggles. We may never be healed. But God does extraordinary things in and through those who are wounded. Even without healing, you may be doing transformational work for God. You may be given insights that are particularly attuned to the limitations and struggles of others. You may become an embodied example of God's grace and compassion in your communities.

Here is the Lord's response to Jeremiah after the prophet laments his pain: "Take back those words, and I'll take you back. Then you'll stand tall before me. Use words truly and well. Don't stoop to cheap whining. Then, but only then, you'll speak for me. Let your words change *them*. Don't change your words to suit them. I'll turn you into a steel wall, a thick steel wall, impregnable" (Jeremiah 15:19-20 MSG).

The Lord's unconditional love and wise purposes are not diminished for those with mental health challenges.

Speak the truth, God says, and do not be afraid to share your story and testimony exactly as you are. You will see God working in your challenges. Others who suffer from similar issues may feel empowered to start sharing as well. You may help create a safe space for honest vulnerability and requests for help. Your openness and courage can lead to a groundswell that exposes needs in churches that others can no longer ignore.

REFLECTION

1. What are the truths and realities that churches and Christians fail to understand when they judge, shame, or ostracize those with mental health disorders?

2. What do we know about how or when God heals? How can living with mental health struggles cultivate the work and beauty of God?

MANIFESTO STATEMENT

REVISITED

As we prepare to close our time, we return to the foundational truth that will guide this study. Please read the Manifesto statement one more time.

Beauty and brokenness coexist in our stories.

Share one example of how beauty and brokenness coexist in your own life, in your family, or in your community.

BENEDICTION

To close this session, read this benediction.

Lord, thank you for loving our minds as much as you love our bodies and souls.
Give us open hearts to see with compassion our own suffering and the suffering of others.
Give us humility to admit when we do not understand, and the courage to pursue truth.
Give us open arms to accept, care for, and support those who struggle with mental health.
Give us persevering hope in your healing and ultimate redemption.
Amen.

APPLICATION ACTIVITY

Before next week's session, listen to the poem "Poquito Más" by Micah Bournes. Afterward, consider and list aspects of beauty and aspects of brokenness that coexist in your life.

Reflect: Are there any particular patterns that you notice? Are there ways in which the beautiful and broken aspects are inextricably linked to one another? How do they come together to create your unique story?

Thank God for every part of your story, and ask God to continue to reveal to you how he is at work in the joyful and painful experiences of your life.

SESSION 3

Myth

DISTORTION OF PEACE

In the last session, we explored the Manifesto statement: "Beauty and brokenness coexist in our stories." We studied the story of a despairing Elijah, and how God tenderly met him with physical, emotional, and spiritual nourishment.

This week, we'll explore the false beliefs and counter-narratives that say we should rely on faith alone—and nothing else—to ensure our mental health. Deconstructing myths can sometimes be uncomfortable, as doing so may challenge our perspectives or what we've been taught. That's okay. We encourage you to lean into the discomfort as you reflect, ask questions, and engage with God. Pay attention to the small nudges of the Spirit through today's Scripture, essay, poem, and discussion times.

INTRODUCTION

"Just pray more."
"Just ask God for healing."
"If you had more faith, you'd get better."

These trite statements are common responses within the church to mental health challenges. Such perspectives fail to understand that our mental health, like our physical health, is often not within our control. We cannot simply will ourselves into health.

These words also fail to take into account the fullness of who God is and how God works. God is not limited by our human ability to believe or pray. The Lord can work at any time through any part of his creation, including other people, medicine, science, and the arts.

Such phrases cast blame and judgment, causing great pain to those already suffering. But God's first response to human suffering is always compassion. As followers of Jesus, we also are called to be compassionate and loving toward those who are struggling or unwell, welcoming them into our communities and sincerely seeking their whole restoration.

MYTH STATEMENT

The Myth statement is a misconception, false teaching, or lie that we frequently hear about mental health. Oftentimes myths sound reasonable. But when we dig deeper, we find that they are rooted in fears, fallacies, or misinformation. It's important for us to acknowledge and deconstruct common myths in order to create space for the truth of God to break through.

Read the following Myth statement. Spend a few minutes discussing why this could be considered a myth. Keep this statement in mind throughout this session.

"Faith is all I need."

SCRIPTURE READING

Psalm 142

Psalm 142 is one of fifty-eight psalms of lament recorded in Scripture. Many were written by David, particularly when he was on the run from King Saul, unjustly persecuted and in constant danger of losing his life. Psalm 142 was written while David hid in a cave with a small band of followers. He was anxious, short on supplies, fearful for his loved ones, and desperate to find safe shelter (1 Samuel 22:1-5).

Read the passage below and then we'll discuss the reflection questions.

With my voice I cry to the LORD;
with my voice I make supplication to the LORD.
I pour out my complaint before him;
I tell my trouble before him.
When my spirit is faint,
you know my way.
In the path where I walk,
they have hidden a trap for me.
Look on my right hand and see:
there is no one who takes notice of me;
no refuge remains to me;
no one cares for me.
I cry to you, O LORD;
I say, "You are my refuge,
my portion in the land of the living."
Listen to my cry,
for I am brought very low.
Save me from my persecutors,
for they are too strong for me.
Bring me out of prison,
so that I may give thanks to your name.
The righteous will surround me,
for you will deal bountifully with me.

REFLECTION

1. What are the complaints and troubles that David is bringing before God? What do you notice about the way David talks to God about his hardships?

2. In your own words, what are the various things David may need to help relieve his despair?

ESSAY EXCERPT

Why is there such a lack of understanding of mental health within the church? Pastor and former social worker Sanghoon Yoo argues that one key reason is a longstanding distrust of science. But science and scientific knowledge are gifts from God for his people to use.

Spend a few minutes reading this excerpt. As you read, circle or underline any sentences or phrases that you find particularly meaningful.

"Treating Mental Health Requires Science and the Church"

BY SANGHOON YOO

In the United States, it takes an average of eleven years for a person to receive mental health treatment after the first appearance of symptoms. The stigma and lack of effective health care systems for those with mental health challenges contribute to this significant delay in treatment.

Long-Held Tensions Between the Church and Science

Historically, the church has sometimes tried to help individuals with mental health struggles. In the thirteenth century in Belgium, for example, the church prayed for those dealing with mental distress.[1] In the eighteenth century, mental health pioneer William Tuke and the Quakers held the York Retreat that modeled humane treatment for psychiatric hospitals, including removing patients' chains and providing a therapeutic environment with food.[2] More recently, the Rick Warren-founded Saddleback Church in California has focused on church mental health ministries, increasing its collaboration with other community organizations.[3]

However, in the last three decades, I have not witnessed widespread church engagement in mental health awareness and treatment. I actually left the field of social work to become a pastor in hopes of serving as a bridge between the church and the mental health field. But I have been frustrated by the antagonism between the two sectors and their ideologies.

In the mental health field, I have seen a prevailing ideology of secular humanism, which denies the existence of God and divine intervention in human lives.[4] The field tends to exclusively emphasize therapies and medications. In ministry, I have often found a lack of understanding of the social sciences, and resistance to the valuable insights provided by psychology, sociology, anthropology, and other fields. The church heavily prioritizes relying on prayer and reading Scripture to overcome mental and emotional hardships. Those who continue struggling are condemned for being weak in faith and mind.

This mistrust between the church and science is not new. In the seventeenth century, the Catholic Church prosecuted Galileo and placed him under house arrest until his death for his belief that the Earth revolves around the sun.[5] In the nineteenth century, renowned Darwinist Thomas Huxley described Christianity as irrational and improbable in the pursuit of knowledge.[6] Sigmund Freud, who developed modern psychology, claimed religion was a childhood neurosis.[7] Twentieth-century American psychologist and Harvard professor B. F. Skinner denied any merit in faith or free will, believing that human behavior is programmed by the interaction between individuals and their environment.[8]

PAUSE & REFLECT

How do you see the long history of mistrust between Christianity and science manifesting today?

An Integrated Approach to Treating Mental Health

As a pastor, I tried to connect faith and science by engaging my church in community projects related to mental health and advocacy. During this same time, however, I experienced my own traumatic season. I was suicidal, experiencing panic attacks and depression, and wanted to give up all relationships and work.

I was then introduced to the trauma-informed care movement, which rescued my life and rejuvenated my ministerial career. I was surprised when a movement leader said, "One of the most powerful factors for recovery from trauma is unconditional love and one person with constant care." ***Unconditional love and one person with constant care.*** These were not medical terms or psychological jargon. This was faith-community language that I used all the time.

The trauma-informed care movement has been greatly informed by the study of adverse childhood experiences (ACEs) and neuroscience development.[9] But the movement has also embraced spiritual practices for healing and recovery.[10] The discovery of such an integrated approach was a huge yet hopeful surprise for me. I am beginning to see more Christian leaders embracing this approach, and I hope many more will.

In trauma-informed care, effective healing and recovery require a safe, consistently caring relationship, and a community that provides belonging and connection. The behaviors triggered by re-traumatization, chemical imbalance, and other mental health struggles need to be understood and accepted by empathetic and compassionate people. This helps those who are suffering to feel safe, understood, accepted, and comforted, accelerating the healing process alongside medication and therapy.

The Role of the Church in Mental Health Healing

Who can provide such unconditionally loving, caring, and non-judgmental relationships and community? I believe that followers of Jesus can. In the Gospels, we see how Jesus formed empathetic relationships with those who needed compassion and healing. Jesus approached the blind, the tax collector, and the Samaritan (foreign and despised) woman, bringing safety with his unconditional love.

I continue to work in the trauma-informed movement, convinced that it can help the church fight the stigma of mental illness and increase resilience through training, biblical truth, and scientific research. The church can be a trauma-informed community, strengthened with these tools and values: safety, trustworthiness and transparency, peer support, collaboration and mutuality, empowerment with choice and voice, and sensitivity to cultural, historical, and gender issues. Through this movement, we can be agents of Christ's love, compassion, and healing to those struggling with their mental health.

REFLECTION

1. How could followers of Jesus promote trust and collaboration between Christianity and science?

2. What barriers would Christian communities need to overcome in order to provide meaningful support to people struggling with their mental health?

"I'm Not Crazy"
BY JOSUÉ CARBALLO-HUERTAS
"I'M NOT CRAZY"
- ALL
(AT SO

POETRY

Poet Tinasha LaRayé challenges the assumptions we often hear in the church about mental health.

Listen to LaRayé's recording of the poem. Then we'll discuss the questions below.

"Whatcha Say"

BY TINASHA LARAYÉ

REFLECTION

1. In this poem, LaRayé compares physical wounds to psychological wounds. Why do you think the two are treated so differently by Christian communities?

2. If Christians and churches are to be, as LaRayé says, "the haven and the vehicle of hope eternal" for mental health, what needs to change? How can this change happen?

BENEDICTION

The ways in which science, genetics, faith, culture, societal norms, and personal experience all intersect with mental health can feel complex and overwhelming. But faithful people have been asking hard questions of God since ancient times, and we know that God loves to impart wisdom upon those who seek it.

Read this prayer by St. Augustine as you conclude this session.

Look upon us, O Lord,
and let all the darkness of our souls
vanish before the beams of thy brightness.
Fill us with holy love,
and open to us the treasures of thy wisdom.
All our desire is known unto thee,
therefore perfect what thou hast begun,
and what thy Spirit has awakened us to ask in prayer.
We seek thy face,
turn thy face unto us and show us thy glory.
Then shall our longing be satisfied,
and our peace shall be perfect.
Amen.

APPLICATION ACTIVITY

Video Interview

Our cultural identities and faith backgrounds can have a significant impact on how we perceive mental health. Watch a ten-minute segment of the interview conducted by Dorcas Cheng-Tozun with therapist George Xiong called "Honor, Shame, Collective Cultures, and Mental Health" from 5:48 to 15:05.

Then spend at least ten minutes journaling your responses to the reflection questions below.

REFLECTION

1. What messages about mental health have you heard from your family, culture, or church? What do you think is at the root of these beliefs?

2. When seeking to care for your own mental health, what aspects of your family and culture do you want to ensure are honored? Are there any aspects that need to be challenged?

SESSION 4

PSALM 94:19

WHEN ANXIETY WAS GREAT WITHIN ME, YOUR CONSOLATION BROUGHT ME JOY

JESUS WEPT

IMMANUEL

EVEN IN THE DARKEST VALLEY YOU ARE WITH ME

Material

EXPRESSIONS OF PEACE

So far we've looked at Manifesto and Myth, exploring a central truth and deconstructing a persistent false belief about mental health. We've seen how beauty and brokenness are very much part of the human condition, including for the people of God throughout the centuries. We've also examined what many Christians fail to understand about mental health and the ways to treat it.

This week we move to the Material path point of our discipleship pathway. We will take a closer look at where mental health shows up in Scripture, and how we can experience the love and presence of God in the midst of mental health struggles.

INTRODUCTION

Remarkably, the writers of the Gospels recorded many instances of Jesus Christ, the Son of God, being emotionally vulnerable. We read again and again how Jesus was moved to compassion (Matthew 9:36; 20:34; Mark 1:41; 6:34; Luke 7:13; John 11:33); he wept (Luke 19:41; John 11:35); he was fatigued (Mark 6:31; John 4:6); he experienced sorrow and anxiety (Matthew 26:37-39; Mark 14:33-34; Luke 19:41; John 13:21).

These narratives demonstrate that Jesus was wholly human and wholly divine while on earth. But they also show us that Jesus truly understands human suffering, including emotional and psychological suffering. When we are brokenhearted, when we can't stop feeling anxious, when we don't have control over our moods and behaviors, Jesus knows what it's like. He is Emmanuel, God with us, present with us in every moment (Isaiah 7:14). He experiences our realities with us. Our pain is his pain. And he offers us the same compassion and care that he extended to others in the Gospels.

We are deeply beloved by God along every step of our mental health journey.

MATERIAL STATEMENT

The Material path point focuses on biblically based truths about mental health. It provides a foundation for us to understand how God sees and responds to our mental health needs.

Read the Material Statement. Keep this statement in mind throughout this session.

Jesus experiences our mental health journey with us.

SCRIPTURE READING
Luke 22:39-46

According to all four Gospels, the night before Jesus' crucifixion was particularly eventful. Jesus celebrated the Passover with his disciples, washed their feet, taught them, instituted the sacrament of Communion, and predicted Judas's betrayal. Then, he spent his final hours of freedom in anguished prayer at the Garden of Gethsemane.

Read the passage below and then we'll discuss the reflection questions.

> *[Jesus] came out and went, as was his custom, to the Mount of Olives, and the disciples followed him. When he reached the place, he said to them, "Pray that you may not come into the time of trial." Then he withdrew from them about a stone's throw, knelt down, and prayed, "Father, if you are willing, remove this cup from me, yet not my will but yours be done." Then an angel from heaven appeared to him and gave him strength. In his anguish he prayed more earnestly, and his sweat became like great drops of blood falling down on the ground. When he got up from prayer, he came to the disciples and found them sleeping because of grief, and he said to them, "Why are you sleeping? Get up and pray that you may not come into the time of trial."*

REFLECTION

1. In this passage, what are the psychological burdens that Jesus is carrying? What are the emotions he is feeling, and how are they impacting his physical body and his actions?

2. Luke writes that the disciples were also full of grief. In what ways does Jesus show his concern for them in the midst of his own suffering?

ESSAY EXCERPT

When we look at the life of Jesus through the lens of mental health, we see how his emotional well-being must have been affected by his experiences. According to theologian and biblical studies professor Andrew Rillera, Jesus' willingness to experience the worst of human suffering not only demonstrates his love for us, but also shows us how complete the redemption of God is.

Take a few minutes to read this excerpt of Rillera's essay. As you read, underline or circle any words or phrases that stick out to you. Then we'll come back together as a group to discuss the reflection questions.

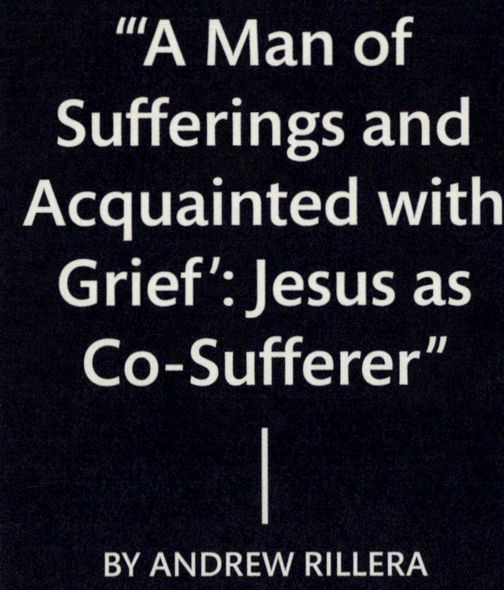

Jesus of Nazareth was a human being. As a confessing Christian, I also believe that Jesus was the incarnation of the God of Abraham, Isaac, and Jacob, who delivered Israel from Egyptian slavery. But just how human was he? How far and deep into the human condition did he enter? And why does this matter for thinking about mental health?

A Man of Sorrows and Anxiety

Many scriptural demonstrations of Jesus' humanity tend to focus on his thirst (John 19:28); hunger (Mark 2:16); exhaustion (Mark 4:35–38); grief at a close friend's death (John 11:33–36); and—it almost goes without saying—actual death (Matthew 27:50; Mark 15:37). But there are other Scriptures that speak to the human experiences of Jesus connected with trauma and mental health. Jesus epitomizes the "suffering servant" in Isaiah 53, who is "a man of sufferings and acquainted with grief" (53:3 my translation).

The author of Hebrews says that Jesus "had to become like his brothers and sisters in every respect, so that he might be a merciful and faithful high priest in the service of God" (2:17). The text is explicit that this meant Jesus' assuming the "weaknesses" of humanity (4:15). The author highlights Jesus' "loud cries and tears" (5:7) and "what he suffered" (5:8). This is likely a reference to Jesus' time of intense, agonizing prayer in Gethsemane, where he reveals that his "soul is very sorrowful" or "extremely agonized" (Matthew 26:38; Mark 14:34 my translation).[1]

Luke even says, "In anguish he prayed feverishly, and his sweat became like great drops of blood" (22:44 my translation). This is a rare but known medical condition called hematidrosis, which occurs when someone is under such extreme stress, fear, or anxiety that capillaries burst and blood intermixes with sweat.[2] Jesus was experiencing painful bodily symptoms of trauma.

This was likely not the first time Jesus was anxious. Jesus began life as a refugee, his parents fleeing to Egypt to avoid Herod's violence (Matthew 2:1–23). Also, Jesus was between age ten to twelve when Judas of Galilee led a failed revolt against Rome in 6 AD. (This is recorded by the historian Josephus and mentioned in Acts 5:37.) His expectations for his adulthood were formed in the crucible of seeing how Rome punished those who spoke of liberation from its empire.

Jesus also saw what happened to John the Baptist, his relative, for proclaiming the politically subversive message of the kingdom of God: imprisonment and beheading. As one claiming to be the Messiah, the King of Israel, Jesus knew his end would likely be crucifixion, the capital punishment reserved for slaves and non-Roman revolutionaries. The brutality of crucifixion also included what we would today call sexual abuse: Jesus was stripped naked, mocked, beaten, and publicly hung naked on a cross.[3]

PAUSE & REFLECT

What is your gut response to Jesus' experience of trauma?

The Salvation in Jesus' Co-Sufferings with Humanity

So, Jesus experienced sexual abuse, profound anxiety, and even a rare trauma response to his agony and anxiety. Why does that matter?

Gregory of Nazianzus helps us understand the importance of the Creator experiencing the depths of all human existence: Jesus' sharing in "our human experiences" is "for our liberation."[4] Gregory goes on: "He has united with himself all that lay under condemnation, in order to release it from condemnation."[5]

It is precisely Jesus' co-suffering with all humanity in our conditions of frailty, grief, abuse, anxiety, and trauma that allows our sufferings to be taken up into God to be healed and liberated. This is in line with Isaiah's "suffering servant," who not only was "a man of sufferings and acquainted with grief" (Isaiah 53:3) but who "bore our griefs himself, and carried our sufferings" (53:4). By his actions, "we are healed" (53:5) (my translations).

If Jesus did not experience human trauma, anxiety, abuse, sorrow, and grief, then those aspects would be left apart from God and unable to be healed, whether that healing happens now or only at the time of the resurrection.

Jesus' co-sufferings reveal that God is not absent in our sufferings.

Our Response to Suffering

Grief, sorrow, and anxieties are the result of existing in this fallen world and being surrounded by tragedy, loss, sin, and abuses. Our trauma and suffering, including our mental health struggles, do not exist because they had some greater purposes and were "good" after all.

Suffering happens for all kinds of reasons, and Scripture names a few of these potential reasons. But Job, Ecclesiastes, Jesus' healings, and Paul's own accounts of his sufferings teach us it is deeply unwise to attempt to answer "why" for each instance of a person's suffering happening at any given moment. For instance, God rebukes Job's friends for trying to explain why Job was suffering. But God praises Job for having the integrity to express how he really feels about his sufferings and his sense of divine abandonment (Job 42:7).

Despite the many questions we may have, the one thing we can be sure of is that God is present with us in our sufferings—even when, like Job, we might feel as if God has abandoned us. This is because, paradoxically, God was in Jesus experiencing the feeling of God-forsakenness as Jesus experienced it (Matthew 24:46; Psalm 22:1).

God takes all these death-dealing things into himself because nothing can separate the Creator from his creation—not even the pain and sorrows brought on by our own and others' sin (Romans 8:35–39). God takes these sorrows into himself and seeks to be with his beloved creations in all their woundedness. Jesus's co-sufferings reveal that God is not absent in our sufferings. God is intimately present in and with our sufferings.

REFLECTION

1. How does focusing on Jesus' psychological and emotional experiences affect your understanding of his work to save and redeem all humanity?

2. If we truly believe that God is with us and understands every aspect of our mental health, how might that change the way we respond to our own suffering? How might it change the way we respond to the mental health struggles of others?

POETRY

In this poem, Salena Marie Scott reflects on how Jesus wept after his good friend Lazarus died (John 11:35).

Listen twice to Scott's reading of her poem. Afterward, we'll discuss the following questions.

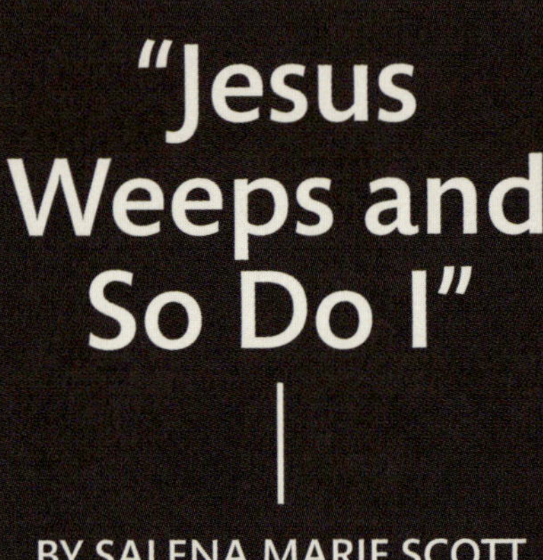

REFLECTION

1. How do you imagine Jesus displayed his emotions, both in this passage and other times when he was deeply grieved? (See Mark 14:33-34; Luke 19:41.)

2. Scott suggests our tears might be a form of communion with God. How does this idea strike you? How might it change the way you see the emotional expression of sorrow and pain?

BENEDICTION

It can be hard to fathom that the almighty, sovereign, uncontainable God would choose to be with us in the messiest, most challenging experiences of our lives. But this is the depth of God's love for us. As Scripture tells us, nothing can separate us from the love of God—not evil, distress, peril, or even our worst mental health conditions.

To close your time, read this prayer from Saint Patrick.

Christ be with me, Christ within me
Christ behind me, Christ before me
Christ beside me, Christ to win me
Christ to comfort me and restore me.
Christ beneath me, Christ above me
Christ in quiet, Christ in danger
Christ in hearts of all that love me
Christ in mouth of friend or stranger.
Amen.

APPLICATION ACTIVITY

Visio Divina

Many of us have established pictures in our head of what Jesus was like. It's helpful to occasionally revisit those pictures as our understanding of Jesus deepens and expands over time. Visual art can powerfully check and challenge our pre-conceptions of Jesus.

This week we'll be practicing visio divina, or "holy seeing." If you are familiar with lectio divina ("holy reading"), visio divina is a similar meditative process but with images instead of text. This is an opportunity to be present to your own thoughts and emotions, and to be present to what the Spirit might be saying to you.

Spend about three minutes viewing this remaking of an ancient church icon by Mondo Scott. Begin by taking a few deep breaths and inviting the Spirit to speak to you. Then, let your eyes wander around the image or settle on particular parts of the image as you feel led. Notice how your heart responds to various details in the image. Listen for what the Spirit may be wanting to say to you about Jesus, mental health, human emotion, and how he empathizes and connects with us.

End your time by thanking the Spirit for being with you.

ARTWORK BY MONDO SCOTT

SESSION 5

WHOLE IN CHR

GIVE YOURSELF GRACE

HEALING TAKES TIME

JESUS + THERAPY

GROW YOUR RESILIENCE IN COMMUNITY

THE SPIRIT HEL
US IN OU
WEAKNE

TAKE EVERY THOUGHT CAPTIVE TO OBEY CHRIST

PRACTICE GRATITUDE

CARING FOR OUR
HEALTH IS A SACRE

MOTION

EMBODIMENT OF PEACE

Over the last four sessions, we've looked at how beauty and brokenness coexist in every person's story. We've challenged the myth that faith in Jesus is the only appropriate response to mental health challenges, and we've meditated on the emotional suffering Jesus experienced and how he co-suffers with us even today.

This session focuses on the Motion path point and how we can respond to what we've learned. We will explore how caring for our mental health is a sacred practice, an integral part of our discipleship and spiritual journey. When we honor our mental health, we honor who God created us to be.

INTRODUCTION

In every account of Jesus' life, he demonstrates a consistent pattern of behavior in between the work of teaching and miracles: He rested. He found solitude. He prayed. He spent time alone with his closest friends (Matthew 14:13, 23; 26:36; Mark 1:35; 6:46; Luke 4:42; 5:16; 6:12; 9:18; 11:1; John 6:15). He had a holistic, balanced approach to ministry.

While Jesus encourages us to work and sacrifice for the sake of the kingdom, he does not ask us to forsake our own well-being in the process. He knows the vulnerabilities of the human mind and body, and he knows that we need rest and care (Matthew 9:36; 11:28). We see the importance of rest from the beginning of the Old Testament, when God himself rests on the seventh day and institutes the Sabbath (Genesis 2:3; Exodus 20:8-11), to the epistles of Paul at the end of the New Testament, in which the apostle encourages us to care for our bodies (1 Corinthians 6:19-20).

When we honor the minds and bodies that God gave us, we honor our Creator God.

MOTION STATEMENT

The final statement in our discipleship pathway, the Motion statement, invites us to embody the truths we have studied.

Read the following statement. Keep this statement in mind during today's session.

Caring for our mental health is a sacred practice.

SCRIPTURE READING
Mark 6:7-13, 30-32

Sometime after beginning his ministry, Jesus officially sends his disciples out to engage in his kingdom work: calling for repentance, healing, and casting out demons. Their work is so effective that word of a new revolution spreads quickly in the region, even to Herod's halls of power. Jesus ensures, however, that their ministry is not just about work.

Read the passage below and then we'll discuss the reflection questions.

[Jesus] called the twelve and began to send them out two by two and gave them authority over the unclean spirits. He ordered them to take nothing for their journey except a staff: no bread, no bag, no money in their belts, but to wear sandals and not to put on two tunics. He said to them, "Wherever you enter a house, stay there until you leave the place. If any place will not welcome you and they refuse to hear you, as you leave, shake off the dust that is on your feet as a testimony against them." So they went out and proclaimed that all should repent. They cast out many demons and anointed with oil many who were sick and cured them. . . .

The apostles gathered around Jesus and told him all that they had done and taught. He said to them, "Come away to a deserted place all by yourselves and rest a while." For many were coming and going, and they had no leisure even to eat. And they went away in the boat to a deserted place by themselves.

REFLECTION

1. What details do you notice in this passage that demonstrate Jesus' care for the mental health and well-being of his disciples?

2. How might you translate the guidance and encouragement of Jesus in this passage into today's context?

ESSAY EXCERPT

We can care for our mental health through therapy, medication, exercise, meditation—and through spiritual practices that are modeled for us in Scripture. Counselor and healing minister Sheila Wise Rowe connects soul care with the building of our resilience in the face of challenges and trauma, and she provides practical recommendations that we can incorporate into our everyday rhythms.

Read through this essay excerpt. Then we'll discuss the reflection questions.

"Caring for Mental Health Grows Our Resilience"

BY SHEILA WISE ROWE

An essential benefit of attending to our mental health is that we become more resilient over time. According to the *Oxford Dictionary*, resilience is the capacity to recover quickly from difficulties or to work through them and bounce back stronger than we were before. Resilience is like a muscle that grows when we bear weight on it. With every step we take to meet a challenge and focus on our mental health, our resilience muscle becomes more robust and flexible. Then we are better able to meet subsequent challenges.

If we look at the experience of the disciples in the Gospels, who together faced the challenge of Jesus' crucifixion, we see both trauma and resilience. The disciples had hoped Jesus would transform their community and the nation of Israel. They didn't understand when Jesus told them who he was and his purpose. As a result, they were stunned when he was arrested and convicted as a criminal. I can only imagine how traumatized they were after witnessing the brutal way that Jesus died.

Neither healing nor resilience grow linearly. Instead, we cycle in and out. We may become weary and wonder if healing will ever occur. But we should extend grace and be patient with ourselves because, as we cycle, healing is happening incrementally.

One way to build resilience is through holistic soul care practices that prioritize our emotional, relational, physical, vocational, and spiritual health. These soul care practices are therapeutic and may be practiced on your own or in community. You can engage in these practices on an ongoing basis, not only when something difficult or painful has occurred.

Engage in listening prayer. Listening prayer is listening with the belief that the Lord speaks all the time through his Word, pictures, the words of others, and memories. Listening prayers can help you identify how you're struggling. It can be how the Holy Spirit brings correction, emotional healing, peace, and comfort.

Bring your thoughts to God. In Philippians 4:8, Paul wrote that "whatever is true, whatever is honorable, whatever is just, whatever is pure, whatever is pleasing, whatever is commendable, if there is any excellence and if there is anything worthy of praise, think about these things." As we listen and are attentive to our story's pain and beauty, our thought life transforms. So, we "take every thought captive to obey Christ" (2 Corinthians 10:5). We can take those nagging thoughts and ask the Lord what he thinks, or for any insight we need to know.

Rely on relationships. Jesus' disciples grew in resilience even as they grieved his death—but they did not do so alone. Through church, support groups, and online or in-person friendships, the support of others helps build our resilience. So does seeing a therapist, journaling, and expressing ourselves through art. These connections remind us that we are stronger and not as alone as we thought.

Care for your body. Practicing relaxation techniques releases energy, tension, and stress. So, walk, dance, stretch, take a nap, and remember to breathe. The word *sabbath* means "to stop, take pause, and be at rest." The Old Testament command to rest is for our benefit. Resting is a revolutionary act, as we surrender our lives solely to the Lord's care. You can also ask Jesus for help in breath prayers: slowly breathe in encouragements, such as "Jesus, your love is perfect," and then exhale what needs to be released—fear, anxiety, stress, and more.

Express gratitude. There is much to be thankful for, even during tough times. The apostle Paul writes, "Do not worry about anything, but in everything by prayer and supplication with thanksgiving let your requests be made known to God" (Philippians 4:6). We can be grateful for minor and major things, and we can bless others by sharing our reflections.

Neither healing nor resilience grow linearly. Instead, we cycle in and out.

Remember to play. Do not deny the hardships, but don't forget to focus on beauty, love, joy, and laughter. Many of us need to enjoy ourselves in the healthy and fun ways that children do. Expressive art and music, or playing board games or video games, can engage us creatively and allow us to connect with God's playful presence without the pressure to impress or perform.

Practice prayerful activism. As we become more resilient, we can better "bear one another's burdens" (Galatians 6:2). The prophet Isaiah calls us to "learn to do good; seek justice, rescue the oppressed, defend the orphan, plead for the widow" (Isaiah 1:17). As we advocate for others, we declare that we trust God to take care of us, and out of his abundance, we have more than enough to bless others.

REFLECTION

1. How can soul care and spiritual practices strengthen our resilience and help us process through trauma and hardship?

2. Of the soul care practices that Rowe outlines, which appeals most to you? Which one might be the hardest for you to practice?

VIDEO REFLECTION

God is always at work in our lives, even during and through our mental health challenges. Watch this three-minute video of PAX team members reflecting on their mental health struggles and how they have been changed as a result.

Then, share with one another how mental health has affected your own personal and spiritual development.

"What Mental Health Challenges Have Taught Us"

BY PAX TEAM

REFLECTION

1. How have you seen God working through your emotional needs?

2. Where would you like to see more of God?

BENEDICTION

Caring for our mental health is a sacred practice, and the more we invite God into the process, the more we can experience God's love, hope, and potential healing.

Close this session by reading this prayer from theologian Howard Thurman.

Open unto me, light for my darkness

Open unto me, courage for my fear

Open unto me, hope for my despair

Open unto me, peace for my turmoil

Open unto me, joy for my sorrow

Open unto me, strength for my weakness

Open unto me, wisdom for my confusion

Open unto me, forgiveness for my sins

Open unto me, tenderness for my toughness

Open unto me, love for my hates

Open unto me, Thy Self for myself

Lord, Lord, open unto me!

Amen.

APPLICATION ACTIVITY

Practicing Soul Care

Within a day or two after completing this session, set aside some time to review the soul care practices that Sheila Wise Rowe outlined in her article. Pick one that you want to try to practice during the week. Try to do this practice at least two or three times before the next session.

Pay attention to the ways in which your emotions, thought patterns, physical sensations, and behaviors may be affected by engaging in this practice.

Thank God for how he can work through simple practices done faithfully.

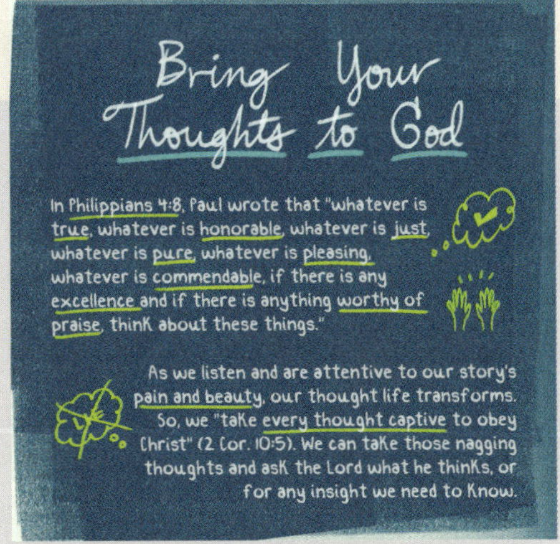

Rely on Relationships

Jesus' disciples grew in resilience even as they grieved his death — but they did not do so alone.

Through church, support groups, and online or in-person friendships, the support of others helps build our resilience. So does seeing a therapist, journaling, and expressing ourselves through art.

These connections remind us that we are stronger and not as alone as we thought. Others can hope for us and help us dream again.

Care for Your Body

Practicing relaxation techniques releases energy, tension, and stress. Our mental and emotional health can become compromised if we are not eating, sleeping, or exercising. So, walk, dance, stretch, take a nap, and remember to breathe.

The word sabbath means to stop, take pause, and be at rest. The Old Testament command to rest is for our benefit. Resting is a revolutionary act, as we surrender our lives solely to the Lord's care. You can also ask Jesus for help in breath prayers: Slowly breathe in encouragements, such as "Jesus, your love is perfect," and then exhale what needs to be released — fear, anxiety, stress, and more.

Express Gratitude

Remembering the highs and lows of our journey is crucial. There is much to be thankful for, even during tough times.

The apostle Paul writes, "Do not worry about anything, but in everything by prayer and supplication with thanksgiving let your requests be made known to God" (Phil. 4:6).

We can be grateful for minor and major things, and we can bless others by sharing our reflections.

ARTWORK BY NATHALIE MAXEY

Remember to Play

Do not deny the hardships, but don't forget to focus on beauty, love, joy, and laughter. Many of us need to enjoy ourselves in the healthy and fun ways that children do.

Expressive art and music, or playing board games or video games, can engage us creatively and allow us to connect with God's playful presence. We can connect with others and our environment without the pressure to impress or perform.

Practice Prayerful Activism

As we become more resilient, we can better "bear one another's burdens" (Gal. 6:2).

The prophet Isaiah calls us to "learn to do good; seek justice, rescue the oppressed, defend the orphan, plead for the widow" (Isa. 1:17).

As we advocate for others, we declare that we trust God to take care of us, and out of his abundance, we have more than enough to bless others. Resilience offers strength to continue to heal emotionally and pursue justice for others.

SESSION 6
closing

We've reached the final session in our six-week study on mental health. In the past five sessions, we've explored mental health in the lives of people in the Bible, including Jesus himself. We've looked at the false beliefs and incorrect assumptions that Christians often make about mental health, and we've seen how God suffers with us in our mental health struggles and desires us to care for ourselves.

In Session 5, we began to look at practical ways our faith and spiritual practices can nurture our mental health. Today we will explore more deeply what it looks like to care for our mental health and the mental health of others as we journey with God.

INTRODUCTION

No matter the magnitude of our mental health challenges, God embraces us fully. Our struggles are recognized with gentle care.

Struggling with mental health does not make us any less in the eyes of God. And it shouldn't in the eyes of the church either. Christian community is meant to be hospitable, nurturing, and grace-filled. Most of us have fallen far short of this calling, clinging to disproven ideas and allowing fear to overcome our love. To embody God's calling as his people is to extend God's love to everyone. This includes those with mental health struggles and conditions, whether diagnosed or not, visible or not.

Despite Christianity's historic failures, there is always hope in Jesus. We can be made anew as individuals, and our communities can be made anew as safe and supportive spaces for people who are struggling with their mental health.

PATH POINT STATEMENTS
Revisited

The path point statements have provided a framework for our learning throughout this study. Let's review the four statements as we process through what we've learned.

Read each statement and then we'll discuss the following questions.

MANIFESTO STATEMENT	Beauty and brokenness coexist in our stories.
MYTH STATEMENT	"Faith is all I need."
MATERIAL STATEMENT	Jesus experiences our mental health journey with us.
MOTION STATEMENT	Caring for our mental health is a sacred practice.

REFLECTION

1. How have your views on mental health, faith, and the church changed over the course of this study?

2. What additional questions do you still have around the topic of mental health? How could you seek out answers to those questions?

CREATING SAFE SPACES

As a whole, the church has a lot of work to do to become safe, welcoming, and healing spaces for people who struggle with mental health. We need to be willing to shift our attitudes, behaviors, and organizational cultures to extend greater care and support to one another. In his guide "Houses of Hope," Reverend Jermine Alberty offers several steps we can take individually and communally to grow our capacity to empathize and care.

Spend time reviewing these steps from Reverend Alberty's guide and consider how you or a community you are a part of could begin to apply this. Use the space in each section to jot down reflections or ideas that come to you.

1. Learn

How do we learn to speak to those with mental illness? The answer is education.

Our honesty, vulnerability, and commitment to learn and equip others to be advocates or champions of mental well-being become the first step in becoming a caring community.

We learn by increasing our mental health literacy. There are many ways to begin an education program with your community, such as inviting a guest speaker or providing educational materials. In the space below, identify ways you can increase your mental health literacy.

2. Live Alive in Christ

The New International Version titles the third chapter of Colossians, "Living as those made alive in Christ." The apostle Paul gives us a five-piece outfit to clothe ourselves in, comprised of compassion, kindness, humility, gentleness, and patience. Love is the thread that holds it all together. If lived out, these six virtues can create a faith community where persons with mental health struggles feel welcomed. We want to embody the virtues listed below rather than the vices that divide us.

- Show compassion *not heartlessness*
- Show kindness *not meanness*
- Show humility *not pride*
- Show gentleness (meekness) *not insensitivity*
- Show patience *not recalcitrance*
- Show love *not hate*

Creating a welcoming and hospitable community requires us to reach out to individuals in a way that allows for the mutual exchange of joys and concerns, where the barriers between "us" and "them" break down. Are there ways that you can extend love to those who struggle with mental illness in your community and beyond? Are there ways you can more fully integrate them into your community?

3. Forgiveness, Empathy, and Advocacy

Why is forgiveness essential to a caring congregation? Because forgiveness is often rooted in empathy.

Empathy is the ability to emotionally understand what other people feel, to see things from their point of view, and to imagine yourself in their place. It is putting yourself in someone else's position and feeling what they must be feeling. Empathy requires maturity. And being compassionate, kind, and forgiving allows us to advocate for the other.

We can advocate for parity for those with mental health challenges in each of these areas. Our advocacy is needed because mental illness is a justice issue. Consider: Are there advocacy organizations or leaders in politics and public health that you could partner with? Are there policies, initiatives, or proposed laws that you could support?

COMMITMENTS

Share some of your thoughts on the "Houses of Hope" guide. Then spend a few minutes sharing how you felt as you thought through the three recommendations. What most interests or excites you? Is there anything that makes you feel anxious or stressed?

Finally, share at least one way in which you could help make your community more loving and supportive for people with mental health conditions. How do you want to encourage one another in these commitments? Is there anything you could do with your group? Write your commitments below.

CLOSING PRAYER

Spend a few minutes in prayer, thanking God for his unconditional love and for his ongoing presence in our hardships. Ask for a heart that reflects God's love, especially for those who are hurting.

Begin and end your prayer time with these words from Psalm 18:1-2:

I love you, O LORD, my strength.
The LORD is my rock, my fortress, and my deliverer,
my God, my rock in whom I take refuge,
my shield, and the horn of my salvation,
my stronghold.

BENEDICTION

God desires wholeness for each of us in our minds, bodies, and spirits. While that may not always be possible in this life, we can still hope and pray for restoration, knowing that our God is a loving, compassionate, and empathic God.

Close your time by praying this prayer, adapted from a prayer by Dr. Tom Reynolds in "Radical Belonging: A Mental Health Sunday Resource for All."

Leader: *Holy One, Creator, God of many tribes and nations*

All: *By every name you are known, you bless the earth!*

Leader: *By your spirit and imagination*

All: *Light the path to right relationships.*

Leader: *Break the stereotypes, banish inaction, bring justice.*

All: *End the long apart-ness that has twisted our souls.*

Leader: *Help us see each other clearly*

All: *And rejoice in one another's strength;*

Leader: *Help us hear each other deeply*

All: *And join in the friendship dance;*

Leader: *Help us guard each other's rights*

All: *And walk long together in good company.*

Leader: *Accompany us as we pledge ourselves to . . .*

All: *Seek to dismantle barriers that prevent the kind of communion you call us to be as your Church, in which people with mental health challenges are full participants. And strive to co-create a culture of mutuality characterized by loving respect, partnership, and belonging among all.*

Leader: *We ask that you would give us courage, creativity, and commitment for our journey.*

All: *Help us keep faith with each other and so with You.*

Leader: *Holy One, Creator, God beyond tribes and nations, beyond barriers that divide, be with us all.*

All: *Amen.*

ADDITIONAL RESOURCES

"Disarming Mental Health Myths: A Gen Z Perspective," a video panel with Josué Carballo-Huertas, Katie Nguyen, and Bek Wright

"Our Minds Reveal the Imago Dei in Times of Struggle" by Jaja Chen

"Where Does My Help Come From? Personal Liturgies for Mental Health," audio recordings by Osheta Moore

"What's the Difference Between Therapists, Pastors, and Spiritual Directors?" a video panel discussion with Bianca Hughes, T. C. Moore, and Sharon Wada

"Nourish to Flourish: How to Develop a Mental Health Care Plan" by Sandhya Oaks

"Finding the Right Counselor: A Guide for BIPOC Communities" by Richard Bowman

NOTES

Session 2: Manifesto

[1]"Mental Illness," National Institute of Mental Health, www.nimh.nih.gov/health/statistics/mental-illness.

[2]"Anxiety Disorders—Facts & Statistics," Anxiety & Depression Association of America, https://adaa.org/understanding-anxiety/facts-statistics.

[3]"You Are Not Alone," National Alliance on Mental Illness, https://nami.org/NAMI/media/NAMI-Media/Infographics/NAMI_YouAreNotAlone_2020_FINAL.pdf.

[4]"Martin Luther: Greatness in the Face of Depression," Wounded Birds Ministry, www.woundedbirdsministry.com/martin-luther-greatness-face-depression/.

[5]"Did You Know that Charles Spurgeon Struggled with Depression?," Crossway, www.crossway.org/articles/did-you-know-that-charles-spurgeon-struggled-with-depression/.

Session 3: Myth

[1]Anne Thériault, "Geel, Belgium Has a Radical Approach to Mental Illness," *Broadview*, September 5, 2019, https://broadview.org/geel-belgium-mental-health/.

[2]"William Tuke," Quakers in the World, www.quakersintheworld.org/quakers-in-action/93/William-Tuke.

[3]Hope for Mental Health, https://hope4mentalhealth.com/.

[4]Phil Zuckerman, "What is Secular Humanism?" *Psychology Today*, February 12, 2020, www.psychologytoday.com/us/blog/the-secular-life/202002/what-is-secular-humanism.

[5]"Galileo Is Accused of Heresy," History.com, November 13, 2009, www.history.com/this-day-in-history/galileo-is-accused-of-heresy.

[6]Van A. Harley, "Huxley's Agnosticism," *Philosophy Now*, 2013, https://philosophynow.org/issues/99/Huxleys_Agnosticism.

[7]Kendra Cherry, "Sigmund Freud's Theories About Religion," Very Well Mind, March 30, 2020, www.verywellmind.com/freud-religion-2795858.

[8]"B. F. Skinner," Wikipedia, https://en.wikipedia.org/wiki/B._F._Skinner.

[9]"Adverse Childhood Experiences (ACEs)," Centers for Disease Control and Prevention, www.cdc.gov/violenceprevention/aces/index.html.

[10]Helen W. Mallon, "Trauma Is a Spiritual Path," Paces Connection, May 3, 2021, www.pacesconnection.com/blog/trauma-is-a-spiritual-path.

Session 4: Material

[1]The adjective used here (περίλυπος, perilypos) conveys being "very sad, deeply grieved" and derives from the noun (περιλυπία, perilypia) meaning "extreme grief."

[2]Saugato Biswas, Trupti Surana, Abhishek De, and Falguni Nag, "A Curious Case of Sweating Blood," National Library of Medicine, Nov-Dec 2013, www.ncbi.nlm.nih.gov/pmc/articles/PMC3827523/.

[3]New Testament scholar Erin Heim discusses this in a two-part podcast series, "Resurrection and the #MeToo Movement"; Part I: https://onscript.study/podcast/erin-heim-with-dru-johnson-resurrection-and-the-metoo-movement-part-1/ and Part II: https://onscript.study/podcast/erin-heim-resurrection-and-the-metoo-movement-part-ii/.

[4]Translation from *On God and Christ*, 94–95. Here is an older but free English translation of Oration 30 from Gregory: https://ccel.org/ccel/schaff/npnf207/npnf207.iii.xvi.html.

[5]Slightly modified translation from *On God and Christ*, 111.

MADE FOR PAX BIBLE STUDIES

MADE FOR PAX

MENTAL HEALTH
A 6-WEEK INTERACTIVE BIBLE STUDY
EXPERIENCING GOD'S CARE FOR OUR MIND, BODY, AND SPIRIT
DORCAS CHENG-TOZUN

MIGRATION
A 6-WEEK INTERACTIVE BIBLE STUDY
EXPERIENCING GOD'S CARE FOR IMMIGRANTS
ALEXIS BUSETTI AND DORCAS CHENG-TOZUN

Let Peace Reign
A 6-Week Interactive Bible Study
Love, Justice, and Dignity in God's Kingdom
Drew Jackson

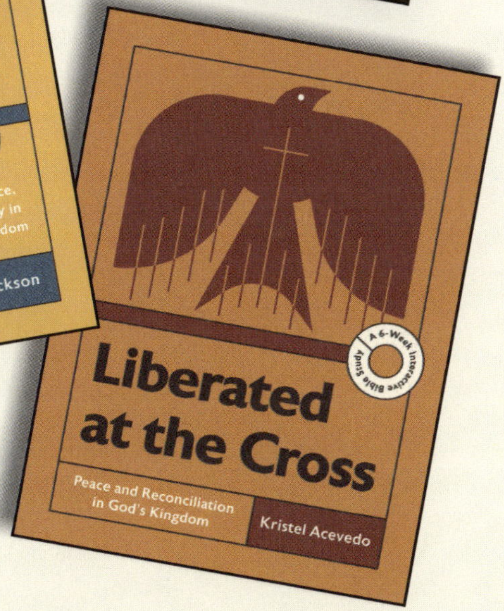

Liberated at the Cross
A 6-Week Interactive Bible Study
Peace and Reconciliation in God's Kingdom
Kristel Acevedo

ALSO AVAILABLE
Liberados en la cruz: Paz y reconciliación en el reino de Dios

Made for PAX provides faith resources by Christians of color and empowers Christians of color through the PAX Fellowship, a nine-month program serving contemplatives, creatives, community builders, and church leaders at the intersection of peace, justice, and contemplation.

To learn more, visit ***www.madeforpax.org***.

MADE FOR PAX